THE Mystery Of CHARACTER

DR. D. K. OLUKOYA

THE MYSTERY OF CHARACTER

© 2013 DR. D. K. OLUKOYA

ISBN: 978-978-920-059-7

Published - May, 2013

Published by:
The Battle Cry Christian Ministries
322, Herbert Macaulay Street, Sabo, Yaba
P. O. Box 12272, Ikeja, Lagos.
www.battlecrystore.com
email: info@battlecrystore.com
customercare@battlecrystore.com
sales@battlecrystore.com
Phone: 0803-304-4239, 01-8044415.

I salute my wonderful wife, Pastor Shade, for her invaluable support in the ministry.

I appreciate her unquantifiable support in the book ministry as the cover designer, art editor and art adviser.

All the Scriptures are from the King James Version

All rights reserved. Reproduction in whole or part without a written permission is prohibited. Printed in Nigeria.

CONTENTS

CHAPTER	PAGE
1. The Mystery Of Character	4-20
2. Your Inner Qualities And Your Impact	21-38
3. Spiritual Sensitivity	39-48
4. Prepare To Meet Your God	49-61

CHAPTER 1

THE Mystery of Character

1Corinthians 4:2 says:
> *Moreover it is required in stewards, that a man be found faithful.*

And Proverbs 22:28 says:
> *Remove not the ancient landmark, which thy fathers have set.*

The Greek word from which character came has a very interesting meaning. It means to cut into or to engrave inside something. It is to mark something deeply, so deeply you can not just rob it off easily. By character we mean individuality. It means the sum of the features and traits that form you as an individual. It means your moral or ethical principle or quality. It is the quality of honesty, fortitude, integrity that can be found in you. It is the sum of everything that you stand for. All those distinctive qualities that make somebody recognisable as a person different from the others is what is called character. It is the combination of outer or inner qualities that you have, that determine the impression people have about you. Your character is your attribute, your disposition, your make-up, your personality. It is those long-term habits that

THE MYSTERY OF CHARACTER

you have continued to express. If there is something missing in our leaders, it is character. It is the result of hundreds of choices you are making gradually and that are turning you to who you are. It is not generally something you were born with and can't change.

THE FOUNDATION

Much of your character is something you create. It is built by how you respond to what happens to you in life. Unfortunately, once character is formed it serves as a solid and lasting foundation upon which you build your life. The real word that makes up your life is your character. The identity that distinguishes you as an individual is your character. When you lose money, nothing is lost. Sometimes when you even lose your health nothing is lost, but when you lose your character, all is lost. That character is what you are in the dark. It is what you are under pressure. A lot of people behave well when there is no problem. But when problem comes, you will see their true character. Character is what you are when you are under temptation. You can be saying you cannot steal but when the opportunity comes and you do not, that is when we know you have a good character.

Character is your real standard at heart. It is living out what you say you believe. Therefore the greatest trouble we have in Christianity now is lack of godly character. Many claim to be born again but they are not. Many come to church but they are far from heaven, as heaven is far from the earth. Many are living their day to day life in deep sin, thinking that the Almighty does not see them. Some go about with strange men and strange women, thinking that the Almighty God does not see things. Some are getting contracts using their body without knowing that they cannot do anything good with that kind of money.

Many are hiring people to sit for exams for them without knowing that it will backfire. This lack of godly character is a real problem. The world is looking for men and women who cannot be bought. There are pastors that are being bought, that are being bribed, who have gone commercial, who do plenty of commercial vigils.

CHARACTER FLAWS

There are pastors like that in MFM. We said, "Don't go to people's houses to hold vigil unless you receive clearance." But a pastor who was around 20 years old and was going for vigil in the house of one woman that was around 42. After sometime it became another vigil. Before you could say, "Jesus is Lord," the woman was pregnant. They ran out of Mountain of Fire and wedded somewhere else. They have been bought and it is very sad.

Sometime ago, I went to minister where there were plenty of rich people. In the end, as I was going to my car, one man came and gave me his complementary card saying that I should see him in his house at 9.00 p.m. the next Friday, to pray for him, that when I come they would "settle" me. I threw the card to the lagoon.

THE DEARTH OF CHARACTER

The world is looking for people who are honest in small things as well as in great ones. It is looking for people who will not compromise with the wrong. It is looking for people who are true friends whether there is problem or no problem. There are some who are your friend only in good times. Once there is trouble, they run away. Those are people of low character. The world is looking for people who are not ashamed or afraid to stand for the truth. Even if that truth is unpopular they would stand by it. The world is looking for people who will say emphatic no and their no will be no; and their yes is emphatic yes. The size of a man is measured by the thing that makes him angry. Anger is a character disorder.

There are many decently dressed mad men today. There are mad pastors, mad ushers and mad choristers who sing one thing and do another. Although reputation is very precious, character is priceless. Only you can damage your character. God is calling for those who would imbibe godly character. When we get to heaven, the Lord will say "Well done." to those who have done well. Well done means that they worked faithfully. To those who have not done well or have worked with deceit, He would say: "Get away from me, you workers of iniquity." They claimed to be working for the Lord, but the Lord would say they were workers of iniquity. Some of the things we deal

THE MYSTERY OF CHARACTER

with at deliverance ground do not need any deliverance at all. A small change in your character and certain things you are doing may be all you need.

Character grows in the garden of experience with the fertilization of example. It cannot be purchased. It cannot be rented. It cannot be imported. In life, men of wealth are envied. Men of power are feared. Men of genius are admired, but only men of character are trusted. You need to build your character.

There was a group in England many years ago called The Quakers. Their messages were not popular at all. People didn't like their sermons because they would ask you to quake in the presence of God. But on market days, when they were in the market, they would finish selling their things before other people because people knew that they sell with the correct weight and would not cheat. Do you have a bad or wicked character? You better repent and get to a level where you can be trusted.

WICKED CHARACTERS

A man drove his wife who was in labour to the hospital and from there he drove to the house of his girl friend instead of staying with his wife. He told the girl friend, "The foolish woman is having another baby." He was a wicked husband. As he drove out with the girl friend armed robbers crossed their way, shot him in two legs and left him. Eventually, he lost his two legs because of his wickedness.

The Yorubas have a proverb that says, "If you have two portions of wickedness, you will use one on yourself." The measure of a man's character is what he will do if he knows that nobody will find him out. A lot of people are afraid of doing terrible things because they know that people will find them out. No man is better than his character. That is why the scarcity of the power of God in any generation is not due to unavailability of people. People are available but the usable materials are not available. There are plenty of men but few husbands and plenty of women but few wives. You need to know that these are the

THE MYSTERY OF CHARACTER

reasons that the enemies are waging war against many of us. This is what gives them the confidence to be fighting. Some people can bear malice for one year. I have seen husbands and wives that did not talk to one another for three years and they were sleeping on the same bed.

Your ability or your brain may get you to the top, but it takes your character to remain there. If your character is bad, somebody who is less talented than you will be given your position. Somebody who is less intelligent than you could be made your boss. I pray that every character disorder that is a ladder to the enemy shall be repaired today by the blood of Jesus, in the name of Jesus.

THE POWER OF CHARACTER

Almost all of us pray that God should change our circumstances but only few people pray that God should change their character. Some, when they open their mouth to talk, lies just flow and they tell the lies boldly. This is a character disorder. Many of us need to pray to God to change us. Jacob wrestled with the angel and the angel touched the hollow of his tigh and broke his long leg which he was using for mischief. The reason God cannot use many people is that there are so many pressure points in their lives which He wants them to sort out, but they are not sorting them out. God works on people point by point, pressure by pressure, and character by character.

There is no amount of riches you can have that can atone for poverty of character. Money does not atone for lack of character. If you want to know the kind of character that people have, watch them when they are quarrelling with other people. When you hear what they are saying you will be baffled because they go to church and call themselves children of God. They have bad character.

Christianity has done you much good if it has changed your character. But your Christianity has not done you much good if it has not straightened out your character. Reputation is what people think about you, but character is what God knows you are. Just as you cannot blame the mirror for your appearance, you cannot blame your circumstances for your character. The company you keep is the indept of your character.

THE MYSTERY OF CHARACTER

You cannot acquire character by dreaming. You must hammer it into yourself, despite the fact that it is not easy. Youth and beauty will fade away but character will remain for ever because it is destiny.

YOUR TRUE IMAGE

What you are in the sight of God is what you truly are. You cannot borrow character. That is why the strength of a nation lies in the character of its citizens. That is why a people will always get the kind of government they deserve. A good character is more valuable than even gold. Ugliness with a good character is better than beauty with a bad character. Because with that your beauty and your bad character you will get nowhere. Your bad character will catch up with you and eventually disgrace you. We need more of good character. God Himself is searching for men and women whose hearts are after Him that He can use.

The Bible says, "The eyes of the Lord goes to and fro looking for men whose hearts are righteous within and once He finds them, He grabs them." You are as close to God as you personally want to be. That is why the Bible says, "The harvest is plenty but the labourers are few."

Now, more than at any other time, we need character than even intellect. No man can climb above the limits of his character. You can't escape your habit, you can only transfer it. Everything in life is a test of character. Though the power for godly character comes from Christ, the responsibility for displaying that character is yours. The grace of God would do nothing to us, if we do nothing to ourselves. God is calling us to perfect our lives.

GODLY QUALITIES

What godly qualities are you building into your life now?

What are you doing now for God to use you? When Mary Slessor came to Nigeria, she was called the Lady With the Lamp. She would take the lamp into the bush hunting for twins. She built a character for her life. We read about Enoch in the Bible. He walked with God. We read about David, a man after God's heart. We read about John the Apostle. The Bible calls him the disciple whom Jesus loved.

THE MYSTERY OF CHARACTER

Will you boldly take your life by the horn and weed out of it characters that are ungodly? Because good character will bring you lasting success. That is why you see some highly talented people fall when they reach a certain level of success, because their character is bad. They are just talented. Success without a good foundation of character is bound for failure. We must pray and engrave godly character into our system. If Joseph had agreed to sleep with Portiphar's wife nobody would have found out. But he would have disgraced his own destiny. Is there any crack in the wall of your life? You better fill the crack today. Is there anything God has been hammering in your ears to change? You better change it now. More than any hindrance to prayers is character disorder.

Talent is a gift but character is a choice. I agree that there are many things in life that we have no control over, like you cannot pick your own parents, you cannot pick your own talent, you cannot pick your own intelligence. But you can choose your character. Your gift may make a way for you but your character will keep you there.

People cannot rise above the limitations of their character. Character is very serious and important because it is the showroom of our lives.

YOUR IMPACT

It is what people see. It is what impacts and influences others. It is what makes the difference to the world. It is the foundation of our future. It is what you put your trust in and how you are thinking, your attitude to things around you. When you look to Egypt for help, you get into more trouble with the Almighty. The good announcement is that Jesus is the ultimate example of character and every time we choose character development we grow more and more into His image. Many have been doing the same thing for years. They have not changed in anyway. This means that something is wrong. Character is more than talking.

Anyone can say I have integrity and respect, but your character determines who you are. Character is who you are when no one is looking at you. Perhaps the trouble is that you are afraid. To be afraid is character disorder, over-ambition is character disorder, getting angry easily is a

THE MYSTERY OF CHARACTER

character disorder. If you are known to be very argumentative it is character disorder. Arrogance is character disorder, and so is childish attitude, if any small thing happens to you, you break down and start crying. If you are always very cowardly and confused, it is character disorder. If you are craft it is character disorder. If you are very critical of people and very cruel or always domineering, these are character disorders. Unfriendly attitude, being very loud, laziness and impoliteness, are all character disorders. Anything in a person's life that does not reflect the image of Christ is character disorder.

THE MYSTERY

The mystery of character therefore is that.
1. It determines your destiny.
2. It can close the gate of heavens against you.
3. It can run you from grace to grass.
4. It can make you a permanent deliverance candidate.
5. It can destroy a relationship that should move your destiny forward.
6. It can make you to miss the Moses who will deliver you.
7. It can turn your friends to your enemies.

8. It can ensure that wherever you go aspiring to greatness becomes difficult.

If you do not address these issues they may do havoc to your destiny.

What do you do?

You need to repent of every character disorder. The enemy has worked hard, caged people and done a thorough analysis of each person. He knows the weaknesses of people and has been working strategically at them. He knows those whose throats are their problems. He knows those whose tommies are their problems. He knows those that pride is their problem, so he plans strategies differently for them. We need to cry to heaven and pray out certain things from our lives. We also need to pray certain things into our lives.

THE MYSTERY OF CHARACTER

PRAYER POINTS

1. I declare that satan and his wicked spirits are under my feet, in the name of Jesus.
2. I claim the victory of the cross for my life today, in Jesus' name.
3. Every satanic foothold in my life, be dismantled by fire, in the name of Jesus.
4. I put off all forms of weakness, in the name of Jesus.
5. Lord Jesus, come into my life by fire, break down every idol and cast out every foe, in the name of Jesus.
6. Every wicked spirit planning to rob me of the will of God, fall down and die, in the name of Jesus.
7. I tear down the stronghold of satan against my life, in the name of Jesus.
8. I smash every plan of satan formed against me, in Jesus' name.
9. I smash the stronghold of satan formed against my body, in the name of Jesus.
10. Lord, let me be the kind of person that would please You, in the name of Jesus.
11. Holy Spirit, bring all the work of resurrection and Pentecost into my life today, in the name of Jesus.

▶ CHAPTER 2

Your Inner Qualities *And Your* **IMPACT**

To make positive impact is to become a force that people would reckon with and not just a mere figurehead. This means that if you want to be a pastor, be a pastor that will make impact; or to be a prophet, be a prophet that will make impact; or to sing, be a singer that will make impact. Any talent you want to use, use it in a way that will positively impact the lives of other people. Fortunately, there is no talent that cannot make you a millionaire, even if it is ordinary dressing people up. People have become millionaires by cat-walking. To make positive impact means to be a source of change.

When the Mountain of Fire and Miracles Ministries started in 1989 other churches laughed at us. Some preached against us. Some people stated that we were praying useless prayers. But those who said so are now praying the same prayers. They are much more aggressive than we are.

To make positive impact is to be an agent of transformation. You make notable impression upon people's hearts and minds when you make a positive impact.

WHY YOU MUST MAKE AN IMPACT

Why must you make a positive impact?

1. You are important to God's plan on earth.
2. You can do much more than what you are doing now.
3. God has deposited great things into your life which must benefit others.
4. You are born as a star and you must shine.
5. Your impact here on earth determines your reward in heaven.
6. You must be a voice and not an echo on earth.
7. You must be a contributor and not just a consumer.
8. You must be among the best and not just among the rest.
9. You will be remembered for the impact you make.
10 You have to make an impact because God is a God of impact. He said, "Go ye into the world and make disciples of me."

THE MYSTERY OF CHARACTER

Jesus was born in a street. That has only 11 houses. Most of His disciples were even born in worse places but they turned the world upside down. They made a change. They made a difference. You will make a change. You will make a difference, in the name of Jesus.

What are the obstacles to people making an impact?

1. **Lack of vision:** Perhaps you have no vision about your life, no vision about what to do. You don't know who you are. You don't know where you are going. You have never prayed "God show me my Joseph's dream." You have never said: "God, let me know who I am. Let me know what I want to become. Let me know what kind of life I should live." The Bible says, "Where there is no vision the people perish." Or you have a low vision of yourself. When you have a low self-steem, a low vision of yourself, you have allowed immorality to bury your star.

2. **Ignorance:** This is a disaster. The Bible says, "You shall know the truth and the truth you know shall set you free". There is power in truth to set free. You must have knowledge.

3. Disconnection from heaven.

4. **Prayerlessness:** Always try to increase your praying time.

5. **Laziness:** This is resting when you are not tired.

6. Pride and arrogance.

7. **Sinfulness:** When you enjoy sin, it will stop you from making an impact. The Bible says, "Flee from any appearance of sin."

8. **Being narrow-minded:** This is an obstacle to making an impact.

9. Moving with the wrong people.

10. Demonic influences.

What are the keys to your making an impact in life?

1. **You must become a friend of God:** If you are not friendly with the Almighty, He cannot help you. Surrender your life completely to Jesus if you have not done so.

THE MYSTERY OF CHARACTER

2. **Let the Bible be your companion:** Be a friend of the Bible. It is recorded in history that those nations where the Bible is their foundation, have never been enslaved.

3. **Live a holy life:** Holiness will move you closer to God. It will bring you good results.

4. **You must be humble:** Humble yourself to learn from anybody.

5. **You must read:** You must read and study. Get good books and materials. Read, learn and study them.

6. **You must have a vision:** With vision you can measure your worth in life and then you will have strength to forge ahead because you know where you are going.

A man and a woman came to me for counselling. The woman became very bitter as she was crying saying: "Look sir, both of us went to Canada to study. I was just 17 years old and this man pushed me into marriage. At 18 I was married. He concluded his education. I did not finish mine." I said, "Madam, it is because you have no vision for your life."

7. **You must seek for competence:** Anything you do, be competent. It is only when you are competent that you will be accepted anywhere you go. You cannot climb higher in life unless you become a master of what you are currently doing. If you took your car to a mechanic once and he spoils it, you will not take it to him again.

8. **You must be a prayer addict:** Your prayer life determines how far you will go in life. You cannot rise higher than your prayer life. If you don't kneel before God, you cannot stand before great people. Nothing must compete with your prayer life. You must bury anything attacking your prayer life.

9. **You must be obedient to God:** God does not want 99 per cent obedience. He wants 100 per cent obedience. The Bible says, "obedience is better than sacrifice."

THE MYSTERY OF CHARACTER

10. **You must seek to live an exemplary life:** You must live a life that others would like to emulate.

11. **You must invest in your personal growth:** You must embark on a life-long journey of personal improvement. Improve your character, disposition and communication. Improve yourself. If people say you talk too much, reduce your talking. If people say you are too aggressive, reduce your aggressiveness. If there is hatred, jealously and envy in your heart, get rid of them. Consign your life to a regular pattern of self-improvement.

12. **Pray for anointing:** Anointing is the power and presence of the Holy Spirit. Without it, you are empty. It is that divine lubricant that makes hard things easy to do. You must receive it. That is why we emphasise the baptism of the Holy Spirit.

13. **You must embrace change:** Change is the essence of life. You need to change when it is necessary. Stagnation is very bad. Change is the only constant thing.

14. **Pursue a life of excellence:** Excellence is a state of quality and achieving it is by choice. If you choose to be excellent in life, you must imbibe the right culture.

With these 14 keys, there is no way that you will not make an impact in your life. With them the Lord will take you from where you are to what He wants you to be. With them you will overtake those who have gone ahead of you.

Deuteronomy 28:13 says:

> *And the LORD shall make thee the head, and not the tail; and thou shalt be above only, and thou shalt not be beneath; if that thou hearken unto the commandments of the LORD thy God, which I command thee this day, to observe and to do them.*

There are 10 categories of people in life. You may decide where you want to belong.

1. **Those who never discover who they are:** Those who are absolutely ignorant about their destiny.

THE MYSTERY OF CHARACTER

A woman, who was one of the 40 wives of a fetish priest, had a dream that her husband came to her and withdrew certain things from her body. From that day she never prospered. Everything she did went down, even her children were not doing well. The woman, who was a Muslim, was passing by our Prayer City one day when she heard, "Die, die" and wondered who was being killed. She then asked one of the ministers to explain to her how we were praying. She asked, "Can prayer be this serious?" The pastor said, "Yes."

She said, "This is what I need," and asked what she should do, how she could join them. They sat her down and told her the way of salvation, ministered to her and she gave her life to Christ. The deliverance minister said, "Go home now, take some personal items and come here because you are going to be here for a week." She did so. When prayer started at the deliverance ground, she started praying. When they gave a break she slept off and had a dream.

In the dream she saw a man in white garment who introduced himself as an angel and came to her with a giant gun. The angel helped her to hold the gun and said, "Begin to shoot" and madam started shooting, shot for a long while and put the gun down. At the end of the deliverance she left for home and on her way home somebody called her and said: "Madam, have you heard that your husband fell sick this morning? He has been asking them to call you." When she stepped inside the room, to her amazement she saw bullet marks all over the body of the man. The man then said: "I was the one who stole your virtue I did not want you to become what you should become. If you save me from this ordeal by begging the man who helped you to shoot to remove the bullets from me, I will go to Abeokuta to get your virtue and give it to you." The woman ran back to the Prayer City. By the second week of the deliverance the witchdoctor was dead and immediately, the woman began to prosper. I pray that every arrangement of darkness to prevent you from going to where the Almighty has ordained for you, shall be buried now, in the name of Jesus.

THE MYSTERY OF CHARACTER

2. **Those who do not know what is happening:** They really do not understand what life is all about.

3. **Those who watch things happening:** They are mere spectators. I pray that men shall gather at your result, in the name of Jesus. I pray that the spectator syndrome will disappear from your life today, in the name of Jesus.

   There were plenty of people by the cross of Jesus when He was on the cross. Some felt sad, some felt sorry for Him. Some went there to sympathise and some to laugh at him. But there was a man on the cross, a thief who looked at Him and said, "Lord, remember me when You get to Your kingdom." Jesus turned to him and said, "Verily, verily, I say unto you, today you will be with me in the kingdom of heaven." Only that thief got a miracle. The rest were spectators.

4. **Those who make things happen:** That is the group the Almighty wants you to belong to.

5. **Those who struggle endlessly:** These are the strugglers and the wrestlers. They struggle to go to school, they struggle to get married, they struggle to get a job, they struggle to live in a house. They do everything through struggling.

I used to have a friend in those days when I was doing my PhD course. He was from Zimbabwe and his name was Sibanda. If I say, "Sibanda, how are you today?" He would say, "Not too bad." When you say, "Not too bad," it means that it is bad. He would go ahead and say, "The struggle continues until victory or defeat or both." As he was confessing in his mouth that was what was happening to him. The strugglers and the wrestlers are just surviving. They have no breakthroughs. I pray that the struggling and wrestling syndrome of your father's house that wants to start painting your destiny black, should be buried now, in the name of Jesus.

6. **There are zero people:** These ones are just there and nothing is happening.

THE MYSTERY OF CHARACTER

7. **We have the "not enough" people:** They have but it is not enough. They are at poverty level.

8. **We have the "just enough" people:** They are on the average.

9. **There are successful people:** These ones have enough.

10. **There are the outstanding or significant people:** These have more than enough and they impact others positively.

Of these 10 groups there are only two groups for you to belong:

1. **Those who make things happen.**
2. **Those who are significant or outstanding.**

These two groups have nothing to do with your background, where you were born, your village or your town. It has nothing to do with the kind of schools you attended. In fact, many people who have prospered tremendously did not prosper using what they learnt. The Lord is calling for people who will catch this fire on time and decide that their lives must make some impact in this generation and in the coming generation. You will become significant. You will make an impact in the name of Jesus.

What do we mean by impact?

We mean forceful effect. It means an indelible mark, a mark that cannot be robbed off. It means making an effect that brings colour.

We sent a pastor abroad to minister. He just talked to people anyhow and did not make any impact there. He was so funny that one day he shouted at one woman from the pulpit asking her why she was sitting with one side of her buttocks. He made no impact.

I sent another pastor abroad. He held the key to the auditorium in his pocket. He would come, open the auditorium, arrange the chairs, take the opening prayer lead the praise worship, take the testimony, read the Bible, sing the special number,

THE MYSTERY OF CHARACTER

preach, call the prayer points after the message, bring out a bag from his pocket and collect the offering, end the service and settle down to do counselling, shut the door, put the key in his pocket and go away. He did not train anybody because he was afraid that if he trained the local people they would take over. He left the place and made no impact. But when you leave a place with honour you have made an impact. When your presence in your family makes an impact, then you are doing the right thing. You are significant. You make things happen.

There are only three things about impact in life.

1. You can have no impact.
2. You can make a negative impact.
3. You can make a positive impact.

I read the story about a cleaner employed in an intensive-care ward of a hospital. It was noticed that every Monday morning almost 70 per cent of patients in the ward would die. They brought all kinds of people to try to salvage the situation but all to no avail. Until somebody discovered that any time the illiterate woman employed to be cleaning the intensive care unit got to a patient and wanted to clean the bed, she disconnected the oxygen. After cleaning the bed she would reconnect it. You can see that woe betide that hospital the day the cleaner was employed because the impact she made there was negative.

PRAYER POINTS

1. Bring quality repentance to the Lord.
2. I shall not be a misfired arrow in the hands of my Maker, in the name of Jesus.
3. Any foundational power, working against my calling, be destroyed, in the name of Jesus.
4. Every yoke working against my spiritual growth in life, be broken, in the name of Jesus.
5. The enemy will not make me a bad example, in the name of Jesus.
6. Every destructive habit designed to waste my calling, die, in the name of Jesus.
7. Power of good finishing, come upon my destiny, in the name of Jesus.

THE MYSTERY OF CHARACTER

8. Every area of incomplete deliverance in my life, receive complete deliverance by fire, in the name of Jesus.
9. Every spiritual cataract, clear away from my vision, in the name of Jesus.
10. Every spirit of slumber, I bury you today, in the name of Jesus.
11. The eagle of my calling shall mount up by the power in the blood of Jesus, in Jesus' name.
12. Every anti-ministry arrow fired into my life, backfire, in the name of Jesus.
13. Holy Ghost fire, destroy all the works of the devil in my life, in the name of Jesus.
14. Every door opened to the enemy of my calling, be closed, in the name of Jesus.
15. Let the waters of life flow into every dead area of my spiritual life, in the name of Jesus.
16. Every weapon fashioned against my high calling, be destroyed, in the name of Jesus.

CHAPTER 3

Spiritual Sensitivity

Sometime ago, I preached a message entitled "The Wicked Shall Bow." I said that three boys went to the farm with their father, who happened to be a thief. He was in the habit of stealing farm products from other people's farms. But before he would start any operation, he would ask his three sons to stand at strategic points to warn him if anyone was coming towards the place. One day, as soon as he sent the boys to watch for him, his youngest son whispered to him that the man should look for someone who would look up and watch God.

You may think you are holy but God who sees you through and through will expose you in due time. There are people who come to the Mountain of Fire and Miracles Ministries but don't know where they are yet. There is no secret of yours that can be covered in this place, no matter how deceptive or hypocritical you are. There is no secret that can be covered permanently. At the end of the day, something will push you out and you make mistakes that will expose you.

CHRONIC LIARS

Why should you call yourself a Christian when you cannot tell the truth as it is? If you have grown spiritually, you will find it difficult to tell a lie. You will require an extra effort to do so. Liars cannot flow in the Spirit of God. The reason is simple: two things cannot flow at the same time. One must stop flowing for the other. Your lies must stop flowing so that the Holy Spirit can flow. Maybe somebody has been trying to commit sin with you and you have resisted the person's advances to a great length, but surprisingly you received the hampers the person sent to you. If you have done that, then you have taken to deception, lie, hypocrisy, half-truth and God cannot but vomit you.

Many Christians are ready to tell lies whenever it is anything concerning money and their temperature will rise rapidly too.

Do you cheat and tell lies in your place of work? Do you take bribes to perform your duty? Or do you take bribe for a duty performed? All these are

THE MYSTERY OF CHARACTER

bad before God, who sent His Son to shed His blood to save you from falsehood and half-truths.

All those that God has entrusted with spiritual responsibilities and gifts should be very careful. A lot of people have turned God's gifts to something they can use to manipulate and control others, God will judge them with greater severity.

If God has deposited a gift in your life, and you are using it to control others in a bad way, you are preparing yourself for His wrath. He will judge you severely. A lot of people have been manipulated terribly by some funny churches and so-called priests, prophets, prophetesses, etc. before they realised the truth.

Spiritual sensitivity and alertness are needed today more than at any time in Christian history. You need to learn how to discern things spiritually. You must be sharp enough spiritually to detect the sound of the alarm of the Almighty.

A time comes when the alarm of the Almighty will sound. However, when it sounds, the possibility of making amends may be over.

When you refuse to expose yourself to God and you cover up deceit, you are planning to be vomited by Him. You must recognise any trait of falsehood in every area of your life.

You must not be the kind of Christian who goes about with a smiling face, but deep down within you, you have an axe. You must carry out the necessary restitution today concerning your lies, deception, pretence and dishonesty. Cry to God to be delivered from them. This is the time to repent and get out of this kind of life, for no secret is hidden before God. You can hide something from the pastor or your parents, because they are human beings and cannot see everything. But a day is coming, when no secret shall be hidden. If you think nobody sees you, you are deceiving yourself.

THE MYSTERY OF CHARACTER

THE DETECTIVE

Unbelievable things have happened to people who are supposed to be standing for the truth. So, it is not time to boast. The Bible says we don't have confidence in the flesh. It must die because it is not going to heaven. It is not interested in heaven. Why does it not want to make it? It is because a curse has been placed upon it: "Dust thou art, and unto the dust thou shall return." So, it already knows where it is going. Most people don't know where they are going. Perhaps you are in the habit of saying that the spirit is willing but the flesh is weak. Have a re-think today.

POSITIVE CONFESSION

We have so many enemies because we run a do-it-yourself ministry. We teach people what to do without necessarily carrying themselves on the ladder of any man. Even if the pastors are not around people will know what to do to solve a particular problem. It is hypocrisy to claim that you believe in something when it is not so. Once God has promised you a particular thing, doubting it is saying that God is telling you a lie.

Numbers 23:19 says:

> *God is not a man that He should lie, neither the son of man that He should repent, hath he said, and shall He not do it? Or hath He spoken and shall not make good.*

Those who take their stand on what God has said focus on it and keep confessing it. They refuse to focus on circumstances. In the midst of challenging circumstances and open turbulence that is so obvious to sight and reason, they keep confessing the word of God. To such people the promise of God will eventually come to pass. But if they fail to confess the word of God, then nothing happens and they make God a liar.

TOTAL FREEDOM

If you do not tell lies but doubt God, you are lying against Him. Faith believes God. It is not moved by circumstances, what the eyes can see, the number of reasons put forward for failure, or by obstacles on the way.

It will damn the consequences and speak the truth. But doubt will disbelieve the Lord. It will question Him. It will agree with your physical eyes and with the opinions of your fellow human beings. It will not only believe and fear circumstances, it will lie against God. It overthrows God's promises and withdraws from His chosen way.

Are you in doubt? If yes, then you are a liar. For you claim to have confidence in God forever, whereas you are not. You must be free from all sorts of lies, deceit, pretence and hypocrisy.

MODERN HYPOCRITES

If you have been trying to cover up with lies, you must repent. Have you lied to others to cover your sins? Then you must repent. Have you exaggerated the blessings from the Lord to exalt yourself?

Some people turn themselves to deceptive prophets or prophetesses. Anytime you meet them they will say, "The Lord gave me a message, the Lord gave me a vision, the Lord gave me a revelation." Meanwhile this same person speaking is a heavy sleeper.

But to sound spiritual and have some respect, he would say, "I receive a word from the Lord." Deception!

Are you living above your experience? Do you pray high sounding prayers, but you are a jelly inside? Maybe you are even struggling with lust, adultery and hypocrisy inside you. Although people are praising God for you but you are nothing. Have you destroyed documents that you know can implicate you when you know you are guilty? Are you the kind of person who will put in your tax form that you have four or seven children which you don't have? Do you state in the form that your parents who were long dead are alive and are your dependants? Lies, hypocrisy and deceit!

PRAYER POINTS

1. Every rusted spiritual pipe in my life, receive wholeness, in the name of Jesus.
2. I command every power eating up my spiritual pipe to be roasted, in the name of Jesus.

THE MYSTERY OF CHARACTER

3. I renounce any evil dedication placed upon my life, in the name of Jesus.
4. I break, every evil edict and ordination, in the name of Jesus.
5. I renounce and loose myself from every negative dedication placed upon my life, in Jesus' name.
6. I command all demons associated with dedication to leave now, in the name of Jesus Christ.
7. I loose myself from any inherited bondage, in the name of Jesus.
8. I break and loose myself from every evil inherited covenant, in the name of Jesus.
9. I break myself from every inherited evil curse, in the name of Jesus.
10. I command all foundational strongmen attached to my life to be paralysed, in the name of Jesus.
11. I cancel the consequences of any evil local name attached to my person, in the name of Jesus.
12. I bind all principalities and powers operating over and within my life, in the name of Jesus.

CHAPTER 4

PREPARE To Meet *Your* GOD

Amos 4:12 says:
> *Therefore thus will I do unto thee, O Israel: and because I will do this unto thee, prepare to meet thy God, O Israel.*

The book of Genesis is filled with lamentable and tragic occurrences. Genesis chapter 19 paints a very terrible picture of life in a place called Sodom and Gomorrah. The city was a symbol of open and shameless pervasion. **Genesis 19:4** says:

> *But before they lay down, the men of the city, even the men of Sodom, compassed the house round, both old and young, all the people from every quarter.*

THE EXPIRY DATE

This verse tells us that some visitors came from heaven to a person and the men of the city wanted to mess them up sexually. Both old and young, all the people of Sodom, were perverse people. The city was overpopulated with strange human beings. Men of this city were involved in all kinds of perverse sexual activities. God watched the city for a while. That is, He gave them a very long rope, but He had an expiry date. Once He gets tired of what you are doing, then trouble starts.

Genesis 18:20 says:

And the LORD said, Because the cry of Sodom and Gomorrah is great, and because their sin is very grievous.

The verdict of God was very clear, because for every sin you commit, a voice is there to cry to heaven. The cry of the sins of Sodom and Gomorrah were so loud in heaven that God arose to deal with the city. Lot and his family were drawn to Sodom. His family lived among these perverse people.

THE BACKSLIDER

The Bible makes it clear that God gave Lot a clear warning to run for his life or else he would be consumed by His wrath. He was told never to look back and never to stop moving because the doom of Sodom and Gomorrah was approaching. The Lord rained fire and brimstone on the city and the corrupt city sank slowly. Lot and his family ran away. However, only the legs of his wife were running away, her heart was not running.

THE MYSTERY OF CHARACTER

Genesis 19:26 says:

> *But his wife looked back from behind him, and she became a pillar of salt.*

Lot's wife looked back and went straight to hell from Sodom. Why did she look behind? Because she was still attached to Sodom and Gomorrah. She wilfully refused to cut off her emotional ties to that city.

Beloved, pulling away from sin may be very difficult, because it has an attraction for the flesh. The people of Sodom and Gomorrah did not take God seriously when they heard that the city was going to be destroyed. But when it happened the mocking turned to screams of terror and death. What killed Lot's wife? What did Jesus say in **Luke 17:32?** He said:

Remember Lot's wife.

Lot's wife died because she saw no need to take God seriously. She knew what God was saying but rejected it. That was why she perished. Although she was the wife of a righteous man and made a good start, she did not finish well. She died in the hands of the angel trying to save her life.

One man who reminds us of impending danger is Lot. Unfortunately, a good number of people face more danger than Lot.

Genesis 19: 1 - 38 says:
> *And there came two angels to Sodom at even; and Lot sat in the gate of Sodom: and Lot seeing them rose up to meet them; and he bowed himself with his face toward the ground; And he said, Behold now, my lords, turn in, I pray you, into your servant's house, and tarry all night, and wash your feet, and ye shall rise up early, and go on your ways. And they said, Nay; but we will abide in the street all night. And he pressed upon them greatly; and they turned in unto him, and entered into his house; and he made them a feast, and did bake unleavened bread, and they did eat. But before they lay down, the men of the city, even the*

THE MYSTERY OF CHARACTER

men of Sodom, compassed the house round, both old and young, all the people from every quarter: And they called unto Lot, and said unto him, Where are the men which came in to thee this night? bring them out unto us, that we may know them. And Lot went out at the door unto them, and shut the door after him, And said, I pray you, brethren, do not so wickedly. Behold now, I have two daughters which have not known man; let me, I pray you, bring them out unto you, and do ye to them as is good in your eyes: only unto these men do nothing; for therefore came they under the shadow of my roof. And they said, Stand back. And they said again, This one fellow came in to sojourn, and he will needs be a judge: now will we deal worse with thee, than with them. And they pressed sore upon the man, even Lot, and came near to break the door. But the men put forth their hand, and pulled Lot into the house to them, and shut to the door. And they smote the men that were at the door of the house with blindness, both small and great: so that they wearied themselves to find the door. And the men said unto Lot, Hast thou here any besides? son in law, and thy sons, and thy daughters, and whatsoever thou hast in the city, bring them out of this place: For we will destroy this place, because the cry of them is waxen great before the face of the LORD; and the LORD hath sent us to destroy it. And Lot went out, and spake unto his sons in law, which married his daughters, and said, Up, get you out of this place; for the LORD will destroy this city. But he seemed as one that mocked unto his sons in law. And when the morning arose, then the angels hastened Lot, saying, Arise, take thy wife, and thy two daughters, which are here; lest thou be consumed in the iniquity of the city. And while he lingered, the men laid hold upon his hand, and upon the hand of his wife, and upon the hand of his two daughters; the LORD being merciful unto him: and they brought him forth, and set him without the city. And it came to pass, when they had brought them forth abroad, that he said, Escape for thy life; look not behind thee, neither stay thou in all the plain; escape to the mountain, lest thou be consumed. And

THE MYSTERY OF CHARACTER

Lot said unto them, Oh, not so, my Lord: Behold now, thy servant hath found grace in thy sight, and thou hast magnified thy mercy, which thou hast shewed unto me in saving my life; and I cannot escape to the mountain, lest some evil take me, and I die: Behold now, this city is near to flee unto, and it is a little one: Oh, let me escape thither, (is it not a little one?) and my soul shall live. And he said unto him, See, I have accepted thee concerning this thing also, that I will not overthrow this city, for the which thou hast spoken. Haste thee, escape thither; for I cannot do any thing till thou be come thither. Therefore the name of the city was called Zoar. The sun was risen upon the earth when Lot entered into Zoar. Then the LORD rained upon Sodom and upon Gomorrah brimstone and fire from the LORD out of heaven; And he overthrew those cities, and all the plain, and all the inhabitants of the cities, and that which grew upon the ground. But his wife looked back from behind him, and she became a pillar of salt. And Abraham gat up early in the morning to the place where he stood before the LORD: And he looked toward Sodom and Gomorrah, and toward all the land of the plain, and beheld, and, lo, the smoke of the country went up as the smoke of a furnace. And it came to pass, when God destroyed the cities of the plain, that God remembered Abraham, and sent Lot out of the midst of the overthrow, when he overthrew the cities in the which Lot dwelt. And Lot went up out of Zoar, and dwelt in the mountain, and his two daughters with him; for he feared to dwell in Zoar: and he dwelt in a cave, he and his two daughters. And the firstborn said unto the younger, Our father is old, and there is not a man in the earth to come in unto us after the manner of all the earth: Come, let us make our father drink wine, and we will lie with him, that we may preserve seed of our father. And they made their father drink wine that night: and the firstborn went in, and lay with her father; and he perceived not when she lay down, nor when she arose. And it came to pass on the morrow, that the firstborn said unto the younger, Behold, I lay yesternight with my father: let us make him drink wine this night also; and go thou in, and lie with him, that we may preserve seed of our Father. And they made their father drink wine that night also: and the younger arose,

THE MYSTERY OF CHARACTER

> *and lay with him; and he perceived not when she lay down, nor when she arose. Thus were both the daughters of Lot with child by their father. And the firstborn bare a son, and called his name Moab: the same is the father of the Moabites unto this day. And the younger, she also bare a son, and called his name Benammi: the same is the father of the children of Ammon unto this day.*

God clearly wanted Lot's deliverance and He announced a very clear evacuation plan for him.

Genesis 19: 15-17 says:

> *And when the morning arose, then the angels hastened Lot, saying, Arise, take thy wife, and thy two daughters, which are here; lest thou be consumed in the iniquity of the city. And while he lingered, the men laid hold upon his hand, and upon the hand of his wife, and upon the hand of his two daughters; the LORD being merciful unto him: and they brought him forth, and set him without the city. And it came to pass, when they had brought them forth abroad, that he said, Escape for thy life;*

> *look not behind thee, neither stay thou in all the plain; escape to the mountain, lest thou be consumed.*

HEAVEN OR HELL

God has been showing people who love Him from their hearts how the end will be. If you have been living a carefree life, like the people of Sodom and Gomorrah, then you will perish. Death is the king of all. It cannot be avoided. But the question is when you die where will you be? When you leave this planet will you leave a footprint and people will remember you to be a child of God. The important thing about death is not death itself, but what follows after it.

There are so many people that God speaks to their heart about what to do and what not to do, but they are not taking God seriously. God has called some people to work on their behaviour but they refuse to listen to Him. People go to church but they don't take God seriously. There are only two ways to die: either in the Lord or outside Him. It is either you are saved or you are not saved, either you are a child of God or you are a child of Satan, either you are headed for heaven or for hell.

THE MYSTERY OF CHARACTER

There is no middle camp. It is either you die as a forsaken sinner or as a forgiven saint. Whether you like it or not, if the rapture does not happen, death will surely come.

BEWARE

A lot of people are not taking God seriously. You may not like what your pastor is saying and you may not believe in the doctrine he is teaching, but please, take God seriously. Because if you don't take Him seriously you can end up perishing like Lot's wife did. She heard what the Lord said but did not take it seriously, and it cost her her life.

A REVELATION

I remember a woman who died and was to be buried by her daughter. Prior to her death she was a high-class prostitute and jumped from one man to the other. When she died her daughter came from abroad with fancy clothes and make-up to burry her. She dressed her with fancy clothes, made her hair and painted her lips. When I got to the place, I asked why she was dressed that way. The daughter said she wanted her to be fancied by the time she got to heaven. I told her that she had arrived hell even before she died. She was surprised and looked at me in a strange way.

On the night of the burial, she had a dream that the trumpet sounded and people were flying; even the fattest person was flying. She noticed she was not flying. She tried to fly but landed back on the floor and she saw her mother beside her. Both of them were not flying.

PRAYER POINTS

1. I receive power to meet the needs of this present generation, in the name of Jesus.
2. All the rough places in my life targeted at my spiritual breakthroughs, be smoothened by the blood of Jesus, in Jeusus' name.
3. Let Your glory, O Lord, overshadow my destiny, in the name of Jesus.
4. I refuse to tarry in the valley of powerlessness, in the name of Jesus.
5. I rise above my roots by the power in the blood of Jesus, in Jesus' name.

OTHER PUBLICATIONS BY DR. D. K. OLUKOYA

1. A-Z of Complete Deliverance
2. Be Prepared
3. Bewitchment must die
4. Biblical Principles of Dream Interpretation
5. Born Great, But Tied Down
6. Breaking Bad Habits
7. Breakthrough Prayers For Business Professionals
8. Brokenness
9. Bringing Down The Power of God
10. Can God Trust You?
11. Command The Morning
12. Consecration Commitment & Loyalty
13. Contending For The Kingdom
14. Connecting to The God of Breakthroughs
15. Criminals In The House Of God
16. Dealing With Hidden Curses
17. Dealing With Local Satanic Technology
18. Dealing With Satanic Exchange
19. Dealing With The Evil Powers Of Your Father's House
20. Dealing With Tropical Demons
21. Dealing With Unprofitable Roots
22. Dealing With Witchcraft Barbers
23. Deliverance By Fire
24. Deliverance From Spirit Husband And Spirit Wife
25. Deliverance From The Limiting Powers
26. Deliverance of The Brain
27. Deliverance Of The Conscience
28. Deliverance Of The Head

OTHER PUBLICATIONS BY DR. D. K. OLUKOYA

29. Deliverance: God's Medicine Bottle
30. Destiny Clinic
31. Destroying Satanic Masks
32. Disgracing Soul Hunters
33. Divine Military Training
34. Divine Yellow Card
35. Dominion Prosperity
36. Drawers Of Power From The Heavenlies
37. Evil Appetite
38. Evil Umbrella
39. Facing Both Ways
40. Failure In The School Of Prayer
41. Fire For Life's Journey
42. For We Wrestle ...
43. Freedom Indeed
44. Holiness Unto The Lord
45. Holy Cry
46. Holy Fever
47. Hour Of Decision
48. How To Obtain Personal Deliverance
49. How To Pray When Surrounded By The Enemies
50. Idols Of The Heart
51. Is This What They Died For?
52. Let God Answer By Fire
53. Limiting God
54. Madness Of The Heart
55. Making Your Way Through The Traffic Jam of Life

OTHER PUBLICATIONS BY DR. D. K. OLUKOYA

56. Meat For Champions
57. Medicine For Winners
58. My Burden For The Church
59. Open Heavens Through Holy Disturbance
60. Overpowering Witchcraft
61. Paralysing The Riders And The Horse
62. Personal Spiritual Check-Up
63. Power Against Coffin Spirits
64. Power Against Destiny Quenchers
65. Power Against Dream Criminals
66. Power Against Local Wickedness
67. Power Against Marine Spirits
68. Power Against Spiritual Terrorists
69. Power Must Change Hands
70. Pray Your Way To Breakthroughs
71. Prayer Is The Battle
72. Prayer Rain
73. Prayer Strategies For Spinsters And Bachelors
74. Prayer To Kill Enchantment
75. Prayer To Make You Fulfil Your Divine Destiny
76. Prayer Warfare Against 70 Mad Spirits
77. Prayers For Open Heavens
78. Prayers To Arrest Satanic Frustration
79. Prayers To Destroy Diseases And Infirmities
80. Prayers To Move From Minimum To Maximum
81. Praying Against The Spirit Of The Valley
82. Praying To Destroy Satanic Roadblocks

OTHER PUBLICATIONS BY DR. D. K. OLUKOYA

83. Praying To Dismantle Witchcraft
84. Principles Of Prayer
85. Release From Destructive Covenants
86. Revoking Evil Decrees
87. Safeguarding Your Home
88. Satanic Diversion Of The Black Race
89. Silencing The Birds Of Darkness
90. Slaves Who Love Their Chains
91. Smite The Enemy And He Will Flee
92. Speaking Destruction Unto The Dark Rivers
93. Spiritual Education
94. Spiritual Growth And Maturity
95. Spiritual Warfare And The Home
96. Strategic Praying
97. Strategy Of Warfare Praying
98. Stop Them Before They Stop You
99. Students In The School Of Fear
100. Symptoms Of Witchcraft Attack
101. The Baptism of Fire
102. The Battle Against The Spirit Of Impossibility
103. The Dinning Table Of Darkness
104. The Enemy Has Done This
105. The Evil Cry Of Your Family Idol
106. The Fire Of Revival
107. The Great Deliverance
108. The Internal Stumbling Block
109. The Lord Is A Man Of War
110. The Mystery Of Mobile Curses
111. The Mystery Of The Mobile Temple
112. The Prayer Eagle

OTHER PUBLICATIONS BY DR. D. K. OLUKOYA

113. The Power of Aggressive Prayer Warriors
114. The Pursuit Of Success
115. The Seasons Of Life
116. The Secrets Of Greatness
117. The Serpentine Enemies
118. The Skeleton In Your Grandfather's Cupboard
119. The Slow Learners
120. The Snake In The Power House
121. The Spirit Of The Crab
122. The star hunters
123. The Star In Your Sky
124. The Terrible Agenda
125. The Tongue Trap
126. The Unconquerable Power
127. The Unlimited God
128. The Vagabond Spirit
129. The Way Of Divine Encounter
130. The Wealth Transfer Agenda
131. Tied Down In The Spirits
132. Too Hot To Handle
133. Turnaround Breakthrough
134. Unprofitable Foundations
135. Vacancy For Mad Prophets
136. Victory Over Satanic Dreams
137. Victory Over Your Greatest Enemies
138. Violent Prayers Against Stubborn Situations
139. War At The Edge Of Breakthroughs

OTHER PUBLICATIONS BY DR. D. K. OLUKOYA

140. Wasting The Wasters
141. Wealth Must Change Hands
142. What You Must Know About The House Fellowship
143. When God Is Silent
144. When the Battle is from Home
145. When The Deliverer Needs Deliverance
146. When Things Get Hard
147. When You Are Knocked Down
148. Where Is Your Faith
149. While Men Slept
150. Woman! Thou Art Loosed.
151. Your Battle And Your Strategy
152. Your Foundation And Destiny
153. Your Mouth And Your Deliverance

OTHER PUBLICATIONS BY DR. D. K. OLUKOYA

YORUBA PUBLICATIONS
1. ADURA AGBAYORI
2. ADURA TI NSI OKE NIDI
3. OJO ADURA

FRENCH PUBLICATIONS
1. PLUIE DE PRIERE
2. ESPIRIT DE VAGABONDAGE
3. EN FINIR AVEC LES FORCES MALEFIQUES DE LA MAISON DE TON PERE
4. QUE l'ENVOUTEMENT PERISSE
5. FRAPPEZ l'ADVERSAIRE ET IL FUIRA
6. COMMENT RECEVIOR LA DELIVRANCE DU MARI ET FEMME DE NUIT
7. CPMMENT SE DELIVRER SOI-MEME
8. POVOIR CONTRE LES TERRORITES SPIRITUEL
9. PRIERE DE PERCEES POUR LES HOMMES D'AFFAIRES
10. PRIER JUSQU'A REMPORTER LA VICTOIRE
11. PRIERES VIOLENTES POUR HUMILIER LES PROBLEMES OPINIATRES
12. PRIERE POUR DETRUIRE LES MALADIES ET INFIRMITES
13. LE COMBAT SPIRITUEL ET LE FOYER
14. BILAN SPIRITUEL PERSONNEL
15. VICTOIRES SUR LES REVES SATANIQUES
16. PRIERES DE COMAT CONTRE 70 ESPIRITS DECHANINES
17. LA DEVIATION SATANIQUE DE LA RACE NOIRE
18. TON COMBAT ET TA STRATEGIE
19. VOTRE FONDEMENT ET VOTRE DESTIN
20. REVOQUER LES DECRETS MALEFIQUES
21. CANTIQUE DES CONTIQUES

OTHER PUBLICATIONS BY DR. D. K. OLUKOYA

22. LE MAUVAIS CRI DES IDOLES
23. QUAND LES CHOSES DEVIENNENT DIFFICILES
24. LES STRATEGIES DE PRIERES POUR LES CELIBATAIRES
25. SE LIBERER DES ALLIANCES MALEFIQUES
26. DEMANTELER LA SORCELLERIE
27. LA DELIVERANCE: LE FLACON DE MEDICAMENT DIEU
28. LA DELIVERANCE DE LA TETE
29. COMMANDER LE MATIN
30. NE GRAND MAIS LIE
31. POUVOIR CONTRE LES DEMOND TROPICAUX
32. LE PROGRAMME DE TRANFERT DE RICHESSE
33. LES ETUDIANTS A l'ECOLE DE LA PEUR
34. L'ETOILE DANS VOTRE CIEL
35. LES SAISONS DE LA VIE
36. FEMME TU ES LIBEREE

ANNUAL 70 DAYS PRAYER AND FASTING PUBLICATIONS

1. Prayers That Bring Miracles
2. Let God Answer By Fire
3. Prayers To Mount With Wings As Eagles
4. Prayers That Bring Explosive Increase
5. Prayers For Open Heavens
6. Prayers To Make You Fulfil Your Divine Destiny
7. Prayers That Make God To Answer And Fight By Fire.

OTHER PUBLICATIONS BY DR. D. K. OLUKOYA

8. Prayers That Bring Unchallengeable Victory And Breakthrough Rainfall Bombardments
9. Prayers That Bring Dominion Prosperity And Uncommon Success
10. Prayers That Bring Power And Overflowing Progress
11. Prayers That Bring Laughter And Enlargement Breakthroughs
12. Prayers That Bring Uncommon Favour And Breakthroughs
13. Prayers That Bring Unprecedented Greatness & Unmatchable Increase
14. Prayers That Bring Awesome Testimonies And Turn Around Breakthroughs.

BOOKS BY PASTOR (MRS) SHADE OLUKOYA

1. Power To Fulfil Your Destiny
2. Principles Of A Successful Marriage
3. The Call of God
4. The Daughters of Phillip
5. When Your Destiny is Under Attack
6. Violence Against Negative Voices
7. Woman of Wonder
8. I Decree An Uncommon Change

OTHER PUBLICATIONS BY DR. D. K. OLUKOYA

The Books, Tapes and CDs (Audio and Video)
All Obtainable At:

- Battle Cry Christian Ministries
  322, Herbert Macaulay Way, Sabo, Yaba, Lagos
  Phone: 01 8044415, 0803 304 4239

- MFM International Bookshop
  13, Olasimbo Street, Onike, Yaba, Lagos

- MFM Prayer City
  Km 12, Lagos/Ibadan Expressway

- 54, Akeju Street, off Shipeolu Street
  Palmgrove, Lagos

- All MFM Churches Nationwide

- All Leading Christian Bookstores

- Battle Cry Christian Ministries
  Abuja Zonal Office & Bookshop
  No 4, Nasarawa Street, Block A, Shop 4, Garki Old Market.
  Phone: 08135865868, 08159103039.

BOOK ORDER

Is there any book written by
Dr. D. K. Olukoya (General Overseer, MFM Ministries)
that you would like to have:

Have you seen his latest books?

To place an order for this End-Time Materials,

Call: 08161229775

Battle Cry Ministries... equipping the saints of God

God bless.

Printed in Great Britain
by Amazon